Aloha

Folk Harp Book

For The Beginners & Advanced Harpists
12 Music, Lyrics, And Legends Of Hawai'i

Created By

Dr. Elithe Manuha'aipo Aguiar Kahn

Collaborating Harpist Pumehana Davis Wadsworth

Arranger Paul H. Hurst

Our Mission
Ko Māua Mana'o Pa'a

Our mission is to immortalize Hawaiian cultural traditions through our music.

First: Selecting and performing Hawaiian compositions (Kani Kapila)

Second: Combining the songs with our narrative tradition (Mo'olelo Pōkole)

Third: Inspire singing as a method of perpetuating of our language and its nuances

Fourth: Infuse and imbue our project with the "Spirit of Aloha."

Love to us all (Aloha Kākou).

Elithe Manuha'aipo Aguiar Kahn PhD

(Harpist, Lyricist, Composer, and Bard)

When people ask me, "why the Harp?" I smile and reflect upon the long journey that brought me to this moment. I begin by saying, "It's my second attempt." It is a personal childhood commitment that yearns to be fulfilled. It was 25 years ago when I first tried to play the harp and in frustration gave up. I took on more than I could handle; going to college, running a business, and writing books on Hawaiian spirituality was definitely an overload. Now that I am retired, I can concentrate on mastering the Harp. I promised myself that I would someday play this magnificent instrument just like that man with those thick black eyebrows and bushy hair.

As a child, Christmas was the most magical time of the year not because of the presents but because of the angelic Christmas music that filled me with contentment. I didn't realize it was the sound of the harp that made me feel so warm, safe, and happy. I was about eight years old when my siblings took me to a movie at the old Pono Theatre on the island of Kaua'i. People were complaining about the price of admission being raised from nine cents to a dime. It was a lot of money back then, but my sisters insisted this movie was "well worth it." They said it was going to be very funny. Me, I would rather have seen a cowboy movie *High Ho Silver...Away!* but then again, a movie is a movie and always better than staying home.

I had no idea what I was in for. I was about to have my first experience watching someone upfront and personal playing a Harp. It was an unforgettable moment. I can't remember the name of the movie, but I will never forget the silly looking man with big bushy eyebrows and a mop of curly hair. I liked him a lot; he didn't speak at all and was quiet just like me. He was funny too; everyone seemed to like him. I made a note of that. Then he sat down behind the most beautiful golden Harp that I had ever seen. It looked just like the kind I imagined that angels played in heaven. I was awestruck. That magical song he played was mesmerizing. It was as if he was playing that song just for me. That song *Beautiful Dreamer* and Harpo Marx captured my heart and defined me as a child. Today the song still inspires me to dream of bigger and brighter things to come like personally writing and arranging harp music. Never in my wildest dreams did I think I would be composing music. I will say, the exercise of writing and arranging harp songs has greatly improved my music comprehension much to the delight of my Kumu (Instructor) Pumehana Wadsworth. Oh, to play as magnificently as she. Speaking of my Kumu...

Pumehana Davis Wadsworth

Kumu Instructor/Harpist Extraordinaire

Before my Kumu Pumehana could walk, she had her hands on a harp. As a baby, she would crawl onto the bottom of her sister's harp learning to stand by pulling herself up on the instrument's large base strings. "I was drawn to it," she said. At the age of seven and inspired by her two sisters, Pumehana began her career in music. Like her siblings, her instrument of choice was the harp. She began her professional career as a harpist at the age of seventeen. Much to her bewilderment, she discovered people found harpists and their instruments intriguing, yet enigmatic. "Teaching people to truly appreciate the nuances of the harp is like trying to teach people a foreign language," she laments. "Getting the audience to hear the music is one thing; getting people to feel the music in their bones is another. People have often said when they hear me play, it is as if my harp is singing to them; it's really my heart."

Pumehana performs weekly at various hotels in Waikiki. She specializes in weddings. Her area of expertise is in researching and playing traditional and unique songs requested by her wedding clients and harp students. Her repertoire is extensively diverse: classical, jazz, rock, swing, and traditional Hawaiian music to name a few. Pumehana finds performing modern hits such as "Beautiful Day" by rock group U2 and "Viva la Vida" by the British Band Coldplay are favorite stress releasing diversions. "I want to be able to play anything I hear," she says. As an accomplished Hawaiian harpist, she has played for foreign dignitaries and numerous celebrities including President and real-estate mogul, Donald Trump. Pumehana is an indigenous native of Hawai'i. She graduated from the Academy of the Pacific in 1985. After attending community college on Oahu, she turned her lifelong relationship with music into a successful 25-year career. She currently lives in Honolulu with her husband David and their two adopted daughters Brooke and Jana.

Paul H. Hurst

Music Arranger, Maestro Extraordinaire

Artistic Biography

Paul H. Hurst is a master of varied musical interests. His talents include concert harpist, pianist, conductor, arranger, orchestrator, voice and piano and composition teacher, pop and jazz artist, director of musical theatre, accompanist, recording artist, and music publisher.

In 2011, I attended my very first International Harp Convention that took place in Canada. As fate would have it, I met Paul Hurst wandering around the volumes of harps that were for sale. I was so excited and in such a state of confusion because I was about to make a purchase. I had narrowed it down to two harps, but I could not make up my mind. Innocence is truly bliss! In comes Paul. I had no idea who I was talking to! Here was a music icon, a virtuoso, and I had unknowingly locked on to him dragging him from room to room! Paul was so kind and friendly. When I asked his opinion on selecting a harp, he graciously complied and sat behind the first of two harps I had in mind. As he played, he instructed me to listen carefully. To what, I wasn't sure, and it must have shown on my face. Paul stopped playing, smiled, and gave me my first lesson on how to choose a harp.

"Listen for the fullness that surrounds the harp," he said. Then he played the same tune on the second harp and I actually could hear the reverberating resonant difference. I asked Paul if he would play a tune for me on one of the bigger harps in the next room. That room was filled with huge concert harps at least 40 different ones ranging from $40,000 in price and beyond. A musical cacophony filled the room as everyone there was trying to play and demonstrate their talents and skills. Paul casually sat behind one of these magnificent beauties and began to softly play "Somewhere Over The Rainbow." OMG! I kid you not, heads turned. The entire room went silent in awe; stillness enveloped the room. It was a mini concert I will never forget. Paul put a lump in my throat, a tear in my eye, and an ache in my heart. His rendition was off the chart! I knew then and there I needed to somehow have him in my life, and my guardian angels made it happen. Since that chance encounter, I have had the privilege to be musically tutored by Paul. He has also graciously consented to arrange my original Hawaiian compositions as well as a few traditional pieces that are included in this music book. Lucky you and Lucky me!

Song Translation Dilemma

The Hawaiian language, like all romantic languages, suffers from an age-old dilemma much of the romantic innuendos and hidden meanings of these songs lose its' poignant feeling in translation. Our main intent is to capture its true essence. To those who are true Kanaka 'Olelō language enthusiasts we ask for tolerance (Mana'o laulā).

Song Selections

What all Harpists will find is the Hawaiian oral traditions are very similar to both the Scott and the Irish. The combination of music and stories were and still are a major cultural source of information and communication. The following songs were carefully selected to showcase the nuances of the Hawaiian culture. The fourth song listed in this collection, Pūpū Hinu Hinu, belongs to the Beamer 'Ohana and gratefully used by special permission.

These two songs focus on historical events

Kai'ulani	The Island Rose
Alas, Kālaupa'pa	Kālaupa'pa Lament

This song offers an insightful herbal remedy and universal gratitude information

Mahalo Nui	Thanksgiving Prayer

This song offers a glimpse into the culture and lifestyle of the indigenous people of Hawai'i.

Pūpū Hinuhinu	Shiny Seashell (Used with Permission)

These two songs are typical of eventful social rumors important enough to "talk story" or sing about which traveled faster than a speeding bullet via the "Coconut Wireless."

Ka Nalo Meli Kula	The Golden Honey Bee
Pō ame Lā	Night and Day

Hawaiian Harp History

The arrival of the first Harp to reach Hawaiian shores remains a mystery. A gazebo built in 1882 for the inauguration of King David Kalakaua and His Queen exhibits an armor shield crest of a harp. The basement of the gazebo houses the Royal Hawaiian Brass Band. Tradition calls for a specific combination of brass instruments along with a percussion section void of string instruments. So why use a harp and not a French horn for adornment? What historical importance did the harp play in the life of the King? Was he a harp enthusiast? Was he acknowledging the presence of Saint Cecilia the patron saint of music? Or was it a clever compromise to appease the strong Christian movement of the time and also honor his secret fellowship? Few people were aware that King David Kalakaua was a 32 degree Free-Mason, and fewer still knew the harp with a broken string was also a symbol of this secret society. A missing string symbolized the phrase "Praise to God." Whatever the reason for its appearance, this tiny harp shield made the harp and its existence officially known to the people of Hawai'i at the coronation of King David Kalakaua and his Queen Kapi'olani in 1882.

But it was not until the mid-1900s that the harp became an instrument of fascination. Harpo Marx single-handedly created a harp sensation and renaissance that spread across America and the Pacific. Harps quickly became a common site and form of entertainment on the Lurline, a luxury Matson ocean liner which sailed from San Francisco to Honolulu on a weekly basis. It was noted that Charles E. King occasionally used the harp as accompaniment. Mr. King holds the distinction of being the most celebrated composer of Hawaiian music during the late 1800s

through the mid-1900s. He used the harp to enhance songs as "Ua like no alike," "Ke kali nei," and "Imi au ia `oe," the latter is featured in this book. The harp, true to its persona, quietly made it ashore making its public debut with the Honolulu Symphony in the mid 1920s with little fanfare. Most Apropos!

Table of Contents

Each music composition includes the bardic tradition of telling a story composed by Dr. Elithe Manuha'aipo Aguiar Kahn. All musical arrangements were created with the help of Harp virtuoso Ms. Pumehana Davis Wadsworth and Grand Maestro Paul H. Hurst

Song List

The Island Rose

It is said…

Princess Kaiʻulani

Sad was the day when the little Princess Kaiʻulani sailed away. It was decided that the little princess who was destined to sit on the throne of the tiny Kingdom of Hawaii receive a formal British education.

The princess, at a tender age of 13, along with her sister Annie, set sail for British Isles. Without a doubt, Kaiʻulani was truly the fairest and most beloved princess of Hawaii nei. She even captured the heart of the famous poet Robert Louis Stevenson. He often spent the afternoon with the little princess and her family. His fondest memory of the princess was watching her play with her sister as they climbed her favorite banyan tree.

On the day of her departure, Robert Louis Stevenson penned a poem to honor the sweet, yet sad occasion, as he watched the ship carrying the little princess slowly disappear over the horizon. Little did he know that he would never see her again. Her fragile health, her sister's death, and her Kingdom stolen, were too much for the grieving princess, who died at the age of 23 of a broken heart.

Solo Harp or Harp & Voice

Kaiʻulani, The Island Rose

Words by Robert Louis Stevenson

Vocal

Harp

1. Forth from her land
2. Her is - land here
3. My Scot - tish is -

to mine she goes the is - land maid the is - land
in south - ern sun will mourn their Ka - iʻu - la - ni
land's far a - way will glit - ter with un - want - ed

rose. Light of heart and fair of face
gone. And I in her dear ban - yan shade
day to cast her once their temp - est by

Compositions and Stories: Elithe Manuhaʻaipo Aguiar Kahn
Composition Collaborator: Harpist Pumehana Davis Wadsworth
Musical Arrangements: Paul H. Hurst
Copyright 2012

Kai'ulani, The Island Rose

a daugh - ter of a dou - ble race.
wait vain - ly for my lit - tle maid.
to smile in Ka - i'u - la - ni eyes.

Ka - i - 'u - la - ni Moi wa - hi - ne.

Ka - i - 'u - la - ni u -

e u - e. Ka - i - 'u -

Compositions and Stories: Elithe Manuha'aipo Aguiar Kahn
Composition Collaborator: Harpist Pumehana Davis Wadsworth
Musical Arrangements: Paul H. Hurst
Copyright 2012

Kai'ulani, The Island Rose 3

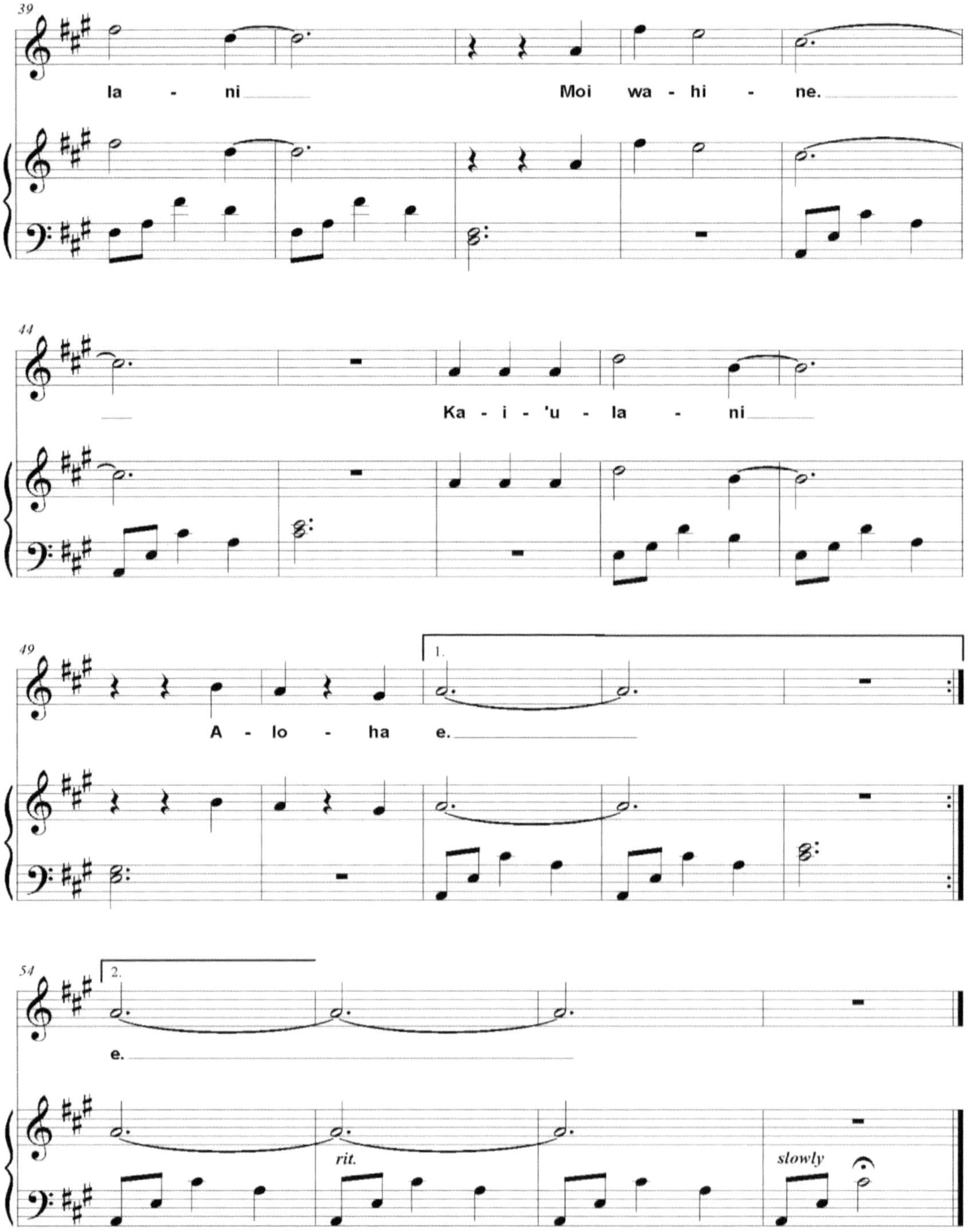

Compositions and Stories: Elithe Manuha'aipo Aguiar Kahn
Composition Collaborator: Harpist Pumehana Davis Wadsworth
Musical Arrangements: Paul H. Hurst
Copyright 2012

The Golden Honey Bee

Ka Nalo Meli Kula

It is Said…

All the animals in Hawaii were invited by the Flower Goddess Lia to celebrate her birthday. This was the moment the honey bee was waiting for. Nalo Meli was new to the forest and wanted so much to impress the Flower Goddess. The little bee humbly presented itself and as a gift, began to hum the most beautiful mesmerizing tune.

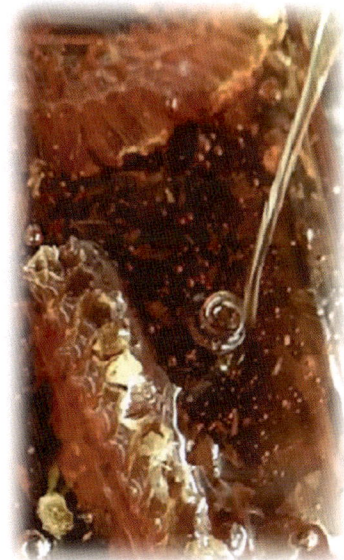

So delighted with its melody, the Goddess asked the honey bee what it wanted in return. "To freely sip the nectar from your beautiful flowers, the honey bee buzzed, so that I may in return gift the people of Hawaii with sweet flowing honey." "You are a perfect example of the meaning of Aloha the Flower Goddess replied, and for your gesture of kindness all the flowers in Hawai'i will welcome your presence."

"But be careful not to use your stinger, the Goddess Lia sternly warned, for if you do… it will surely cost you your life."

Solo Harp or Harp & Voice

The Golden Honey Bee

Vocal / Harp

Lyrics:
The gold-en hon-ey bee _____ wings from tree to tree. A gift from God for you and me, the gold-en hon-ey bee. _____ Flow-ers lift their eyes _____ face up to the

Compositions and Stories: Elithe Manuha'aipo Aguiar Kahn
Composition Collaborator: Harpist Pumehana Davis Wadsworth
Musical Arrangements: Paul H. Hurst
Copyright 2012

2

The Golden Honey Bee

skies.   The gold-en bee goes zip-ping,___ sip-ping

hon-ey as she flies.___   Ev-'ry lit-tle__ place on earth   where

hon-ey bees are   found   you'll find sweet hon-ey   and chew-ing wax

ming-led with the sound   of the gold-en hon-ey

Compositions and Stories: Elithe Manuha'aipo Aguiar Kahn
Composition Collaborator: Harpist Pumehana Davis Wadsworth
Musical Arrangements: Paul H. Hurst
Copyright 2012

The Golden Honey Bee 3

39
bee, with a gift for you and me: sweet
44
nec - tar from the flowers and trees,
LH
the gold - en hon - ey
Glissando
RH
48
bee. The gold - en hon - ey bee.
53
LH
LH
LH
LH
Glissando
RH
RH
slower
play low on string
"stinger" (a musical term meaning the last low note)

Compositions and Stories: Elithe Manuha'aipo Aguiar Kahn
Composition Collaborator: Harpist Pumehana Davis Wadsworth
Musical Arrangements: Paul H. Hurst
Copyright 2012

Mahalo Nui

It is said…

Hokula'a, hated to tend the family sea salt beds at Mānā. "Why me;" Hokula'a complained. Tutu replied, "Our family has been honored to malama, to tend and care for these sacred sea salt beds. We have much to be thankful for."

"Why is this place sacred? It looks like dirty salt to me." "Ae, yes, that is why it is so sacred," Tutu continued. "Do you know your name tells the story of our existence," Tutu said, as she picked up a crystallized piece of salt that looked like the backbone of a prehistoric animal. "Look to the source," (Nana I ke kumu) she said. "You see this? All the stars in the sky are made of salt crystals." Then Tutu picked up some red dirt that formed the banks of the salt beds and fondled it with her fingers. "This is the other half of the story. Mix them together and you have humanity (Nui manu). You and I are both made up of the dust of the stars and the dirt of this land."

"Not," Hokula'a expressed, half believing Tutu. "Ae, yes my child, and because of this fact we must eat sea salt to sustain our life, she said. Our family ('Ohana) was blessed with the honor of sustaining the lives of our people. Without salt we could not dry and preserve our food for the lean times. Without salt we could not clean and purge our stomachs ('Ōpū). Without salt our children (keiki) could suffer deformities. Without salt our teeth (niho) would fall out and we would age before our time. Without salt we could not spiritually cleanse and bless our homes and ourselves."

"Enough Tutu," the boy said, nodding his head fully enlightened. "Give me the rake, let me finish the job." That day, Hokula'a grew into his name… Sacred Stardust.

Solo Harp or Harp & Voice

Mahalo Nui

Lyrics (under vocal line):
Ma - ha - lo Nu - i _____ i ka la _____ i ka ma - hi - na _____ a - me na - ho - ku. Ma - ha - lo

Compositions and Stories: Elithe Manuha'aipo Aguiar Kahn
Composition Collaborator: Harpist Pumehana Davis Wadsworth
Musical Arrangements: Paul H. Hurst
Copyright 2012

2

Mahalo Nui

nu - i, Ma - ha - lo nu - i i ka a -

i - na, i ka mo - a - na i laa

lau la - pu - au Ma - ha - lo nu - i.

Ho - o Po - mai - ka'i Ho - o Po - mai -

roll all chords

Compositions and Stories: Elithe Manuha'aipo Aguiar Kahn
Composition Collaborator: Harpist Pumehana Davis Wadsworth
Musical Arrangements: Paul H. Hurst
Copyright 2012

Mahalo Nui

ka'i   Ho-o   Po - Mai - ka'i   ha-na-hou.   Ho-o

Po - mai - ka'i   Ho-o   Po - mai - ka'i   Ho-o   Po - mai - ka'i   no Ka-

kou.   Ma - ha - lo   nu - i.

LH

rit.

Compositions and Stories: Elithe Manuha'aipo Aguiar Kahn
Composition Collaborator: Harpist Pumehana Davis Wadsworth
Musical Arrangements: Paul H. Hurst
Copyright 2012

Pūpū Hinuhinu

It is said…

There is a game that little children in Hawaii play that is spiritually profound. No one knows who, or when this profound Huna teaching of piercing the "mystic veil" began (Amama ua noa). Its origins, though a mystery, was a factual matter of practice. It allowed children and grown-ups alike to readily communicate with their ancestral guardians. In order to accomplish this one must learn to "Noho pu," to sit as still as a seashell on the beach, silently contemplating and listening intently for the inner voice of our elders (Kupuna).

It is believed the voices of our ancestors who spoke of pure truth and love could be found by closing the eyes and holding a seashell against the ear. The mesmerizing sound of the eternal sea emanating from the seashell will lull the busy mind into a sleepy peaceful state. It is in this semi waking dream state that our ancestors, our Kupuna from beyond the mystic veil, can spiritually communicate with us. A word to the wise… be mindful…don't fall asleep! Pūpū Hinuhinu is a favorite little song used by Kumu hula (dance instructors) to introduce children to the traditional spiritual practice of meditative contemplation (Noho Pu). If you listen you will hear!

Pūpū Hinuhinu is <u>composed by Helen Desha Beamer</u>; Beamer compositions are used by permission of Mahi Beamer, Marmionett Kaaihue and Gaye Beamer. (Mahalo Nui)

Solo Harp or Harp & Voice

Pūpū Hinuhinu

Musical Arrangement:
Paul H. Hurst

Vocal

Harp

Pu - pu

(echo)

Hi - nu hi - nu   pu pu   hi - nu hi - nu   e a ke

ka - ha - kai   ka - ha - kai   e_____   pu pu   hi - nu hin - nu   e.

Pu pu   Hi - nu hi - nu   pu pu

(echo)

Pūpū Hinuhinu is composed by Helen Desha Beamer. Beamer compositions
are used with permission from Mahi Beamer, Marmionett Kaaihue and Gaye Beamer.
Copyright 2012

2

Pūpū Hinuhinu

hi - nu hi - nu e   e lo - he ke - kou e_____ pu   pu   hi - nu hin - nu

e.   Pu   pu   Hi - nu hi - nu
                                              RH

                                              LH

pu pu   hi - nu hi - nu e   a   mo - a   a   mo - e pu

(echo)

pu   hi - nu hin - nu   e.

rit.

**Pūpū Hinuhinu is composed by Helen Desha Beamer. Beamer compositions
are used with permission from Mahi Beamer, Marmionett Kaaihue and Gaye Beamer.
Copyright 2012**

Pō ame Lā

(Night and Day)

It is said...

In the misty shadows of the Koʻolau, two lovers kissed, one day. It was to be their last embrace, for he was being sent away. Tears rolled down the maidens' cheeks, their love was not to be. For she was just a common girl, and He, he was a Royalty. As they parted, she sang a song, and sent him on his way. The Koʻolau winds still swirl this song unto this very day.

Forbidden love

The most common romantic Hawaiian thyme.

Solo Harp or Voice & Harp

Pō ame Lā

Compositions and Stories: Elithe Manuhaʻaipo Aguiar Kahn
Composition Collaborator: Harpist Pumehana Davis Wadsworth
Musical Arrangements: Paul H. Hurst
Copyright 2012

Pō ame Lā

10
Up - on the winds I'll blow a kiss and send it on its' way
14
to touch your lips when ev' - ning falls and to warm your heart by
rit.
17
day.
Po a - me La, night and
a tempo

Compositions and Stories: Elithe Manuha'aipo Aguiar Kahn
Composition Collaborator: Harpist Pumehana Davis Wadsworth
Musical Arrangements: Paul H. Hurst
Copyright 2012

Pō ame Lā

22
day, you'll al-ways be on my mind.
27
Po a - me La, night and day, you'll al-ways
p
32
be on my mind. You'll al-ways be on my
37
mind.
rit.
pp
mp

Compositions and Stories: Elithe Manuha'aipo Aguiar Kahn
Composition Collaborator: Harpist Pumehana Davis Wadsworth
Musical Arrangements: Paul H. Hurst
Copyright 2012

Kālaupaʻpa Lament

It is said…

On still, dark, and quiet nights, ships that sail past the coastline of Kalaupapa on the island of Molokaʻi often hear babies crying in the darkness. These chilling sounds are said to be the voices of babies that were torn from their wailing mothers' arms and shipped to Kalaupapa with other afflicted victims stricken with the horrible contagious, "pake make" disease that ravished the native population during the late 1800s. In hopes of containing the disease, anyone who showed signs this leprous plague was shipped to the isolated and desolate Kalaupapa peninsula. Fearful sea captains and sailors cast the victims overboard forcing them to swim to shore; the old, the feeble, the weak, and the little ones too. Those who didn't make it were lucky. The village of the damned was a living hell. A doomed lifestyle of lawlessness, violence, and filthy starving conditions awaited the survivors. Those who tried to escape the misery of Kalaupapa by scaling the cliffs of Kalawao were immediately hunted down and forced to return or shot on sight.

Then, a ray of love and hope came to Kalaupapa in the form of Father Damien. For years this lone, courageous, Catholic priest chose to minister and live among the afflicted. Physically and spiritually, Father Damien nurtured his flock of "broken birds." He established law and order and stabilized the deplorable conditions. But, ʻUe, (alas) he too was stricken with the deadly "pake make" disease. It is for him and his flock of broken birds that this soulful lament is dedicated. ʻUe ʻue, Alas… Kalaupapa!

Harp Solo or Harp & Voice

Alas Kālaupaʻpa

Vocal

E lo-he l   a - u ka - na - lo____
E lo-he l   a - u ka - na - lo____

Harp

Like a dirge

___ Nu - i   Ma - nu   o   Ka - lau - pa - pa_____   e   hea   e hea
___ Nu - i   Ma - nu   o   Ka - lau - pa - pa_____   e   laua   e

a - na l - a - u_____   mai   Mo - lo - ka - i.
ka - ni kau - me - le_____   mai   Mo - lo - ka - i.

U - e   U - e   Ka - lau - pa - pa_____   U - e   a - na

Compositions and Stories: Elithe Manuhaʻaipo Aguiar Kahn
Composition Collaborator: Harpist Pumehana Davis Wadsworth
Musical Arrangements: Paul H. Hurst
Copyright 2012

2

Alas Kālaupaʻpa

no Ka-la - wa - o. U-e U-e Ka-lau - pa - pa

U-e a - na no Ka-la - wao. U-e a - na

no U-e a - na no U-e a - na no Ka-la-wao.

U - e U - e U - e

Compositions and Stories: Elithe Manuhaʻaipo Aguiar Kahn
Composition Collaborator: Harpist Pumehana Davis Wadsworth
Musical Arrangements: Paul H. Hurst
Copyright 2012

About the Composer Harpist

Dr. Elithe Manuhaʻaipo Aguiar Kahn is the resident harp therapist at Nuʻuanu Hale on the island of Oʻahu. Like "Joseph's Coat of Many Colors," she is multi-faceted, blessed with the gift of sharing valuable and fascinating information through native storytelling traditions (Moʻolelo Pōkole). She is the author of various books based on Hawaiian history, lifestyle, and spirituality. Her passions are spiritual counseling, lunar astrology, research, writing, storytelling, gardening, composing music, and playing the harp. She holds numerous academic degrees; but above all, she highly values her Certified Therapeutic Harp Practitioners Certificate.

When asked about her experience to learn and play the harp, Dr. Kahn candidly replied, "It was extremely challenging, yet a most personally rewarding experience. Playing the harp benefits both the listener and practitioner. Harp music stabilizes and heals by melodiously painting pictures with its healing tones. The sound of the instrument soothes the savage beast within and eases the weary soul." Currently, she is working on a Hawaiian astrological and lunar forecasting system. When she is not traveling abroad, she counsels at Hawaiʻi Pacific Healing Center in Honolulu, Hawaiʻi.

Other Works

"HĀ Breathe!" The Voice of the Shell Sounds, *ʻOu Ka Leo O ka Pū*
"Hoʻonaka" When the Plant Quivers, *Legends of Hawaiian Plants*
"Hoʻolei" The Psychology of Hawaiian Divination, *Activating the Third Eye*
"If Feet Could Talk" Lomi Wāwae, *A Healing Art, Hawaiian Foot Therapy*
"Aloha" *Folk Harp Music Book*
"MU" Descendants, *Living Aloha, Living Love, Origins of Hawaiian Spirituality, Remnants of Lemuria*
"Lani Goose Legends of the Big Island of Hawaiʻi" Stories, Audio, Coloring Book
"Lani Goose Legends of Kauai" Stories, Audio, Coloring Book
"Lani Goose Legends of Maui" Stories, Audio, Coloring Book
"Lani Goose Legends of Oahu" Stories, Audio, Coloring Book"
"Lani Goose Sings" for Hawaii's Children, Sixteen Songs, Audio & Harp Sheet Music
"Rainbow Blessings & Pearls of Wisdom" *Self-help Pictorials*

Credentials

Ph.D. Philosophy in Metaphysics: American Institute of Holistic Theology
M.S. Master of Science in Metaphysics: American Institute of Holistic Theology
B.A. Degree in Psychology: Hawaiʻi Pacific University
A.A. Degree in Liberal Arts: University of Hawaiʻi
C.S.C. Certified Spiritual Counselor: Hawaii Pacific Healing Center
C.T.H.P. Certified Therapeutic Harp Practitioner
Hypnotherapist: Omni Hypnosis Training Center
Credentials of Ministry: Universal Life Church

Mahalo Piha

Thank you ever so much for purchasing this music book.
For samples of our works, visit our website: www.elithekahn.com

A hoʻi aʻe au
Until We Meet Again

Printed in Great Britain
by Amazon